Reading Works

Reading Worksheets is a book of 44 photocopy masters designed for use with adults who are improving their reading skills.

Each page contains a short piece of everyday reading matter followed by questions and exercises which test the reader's understanding and develop reading skills. The book as a whole contains a wide variety of exercises but almost all the worksheets include a set of comprehension questions in a standard format *(True/False/Maybe* or *Yes/No/Don't know)*. Increasing familiarity with these formats and the fact that many words and phrases are regularly repeated should make it easier for students to use the worksheets independently. The majority of the exercises require little writing or spelling skill and even those which do could be tackled orally.

The order in which the worksheets are arranged in the book should be regarded only as a very rough guide to their level of difficulty. The reader's individual interests and needs should dictate the suitability of a particular worksheet. Students with very limited reading ability should be able to attempt parts of many of the worksheets with the support of a tutor. An index of some of the main topics covered in the worksheets is included in addition to the list of contents.

No answers are given for the exercises because they can usually be found in the text itself. Sometimes the answer is open to debate and may depend on an ability to read between the lines or to apply personal knowledge of a topic. In a few cases, readers may need to refer to a standard reference book such as a dictionary, thesaurus or atlas.

The material in *Reading Worksheets* could be used as evidence of achievement for the Reading Units of Foundation and Stage 1 of the City and Guilds Communication Skills (Wordpower) Certificate 3793.

Please read the copyright / photocopying restrictions below.

Publishers: Brown and Brown,
               Keeper's Cottage,
               Westward,
               Wigton
               Cumbria CA7 8NQ
               Tel. 06973 42915

Acknowledgements

The publishers would like to thank the following for permission to reproduce items or for help in providing material for this book:

A.J. Eves Ltd., Chemist, Wigton, *p.9*; Department of Employment, *pp.13,37,45*; Cumberland Infirmary, Carlisle, *pp.14,29*; Linda Lever, Windmill Wholefoods, Liverpool, *p.16*; Belle Vue Veterinary Practice, Wigton, *p.21*; Elaine Yates, *p.27*; Housing Benefit Office, *p.31*; East Cumbria Health Authority, *pp.32,43*; Wigton Video Centre, *p.38*; Monica Whitson, *p.39*; Norweb, Carlisle, *p.46*.

Alan Jackson's poem, *Goldfish*, *p.15*, appears in *Strictly Private*, ed. Roger McGough, pub. Puffin Books.

First published 1993

ISBN 1 870596 42 0

Printed by Reed's Ltd., Penrith, Cumbria on Corona 100% recycled paper and SylvanCoat 90% recycled card.

Contents

Railway Station signs

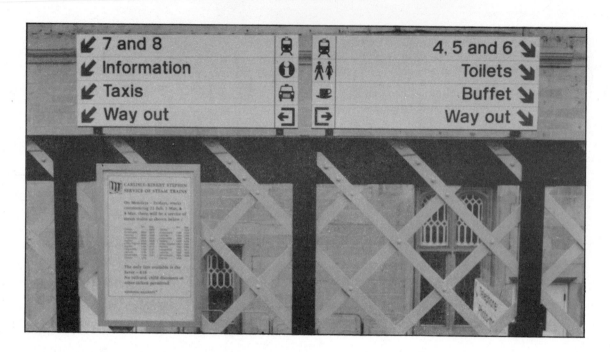

A True / False / Maybe

1. Platform 8 is down to the left.
2. Platform 5 is down to the right.
3. Information is down to the right.
4. The buffet is down to the left.
5. The way out is down to the right and left.
6. The toilets are down to the left.
7. The signs are on a bridge over the platforms.
8. Platforms 1, 2 and 3 are behind you.

B Match the symbols to the words

Way out (right)   **Toilets**   **Buffet**   **Taxis**

Platforms   **Information**   **Way out** (left)

a   b   c   d   e   f   g

Brown and Brown / Reading Worksheets

Small ad.

FOR SALE   3 ft bed, grey metal frame, with mattress, used only twice as guest bed, cost £140, sell for £50.   Tel. 350319

A True / False / Maybe

1. The bed is brand new.

2. The mattress is grey.

3. The frame is metal.

4. The sale price is £90 less than the cost price.

5. The bed has been used by 2 guests.

B Fill in the missing words in these sentences

1. A 3 ft bed is ____ sale.

2. The bed has only been used ____.

3. The ____ cost £140 when new.

4. The bed has a mattress ____ a grey metal frame.

C How many?

1. How many words in the ad. begin with **f** ?

2. How many words in the ad. end in **e** ?

3. How many words in the ad. have **s** in them?

4. How many numbers are there in the ad.?

A note on the door

a
Telecom

Key at N⁰. 38 →

b
Telecom

Key under mat.

c
Telecom

Back in 10 minutes

d
Telecom
Had to go out.
Come back tomorrow.

A True / False / Maybe

1. Telecom are coming to mend the phone.
2. The person in the flat is out.
3. The door is locked.
4. All the notes could help a burglar.
5. No. 38 is to the right.

B What do you think?

1. Which notes let Telecom get into the flat at once?
2. Which note means that Telecom will have to wait to get in?
3. Which note means that Telecom will not get in today?
4. Which note is the best one for a burglar to see?
5. Which note shows that a neighbour is trusted?
6. Which note, if any, would you leave on your door?

Street map

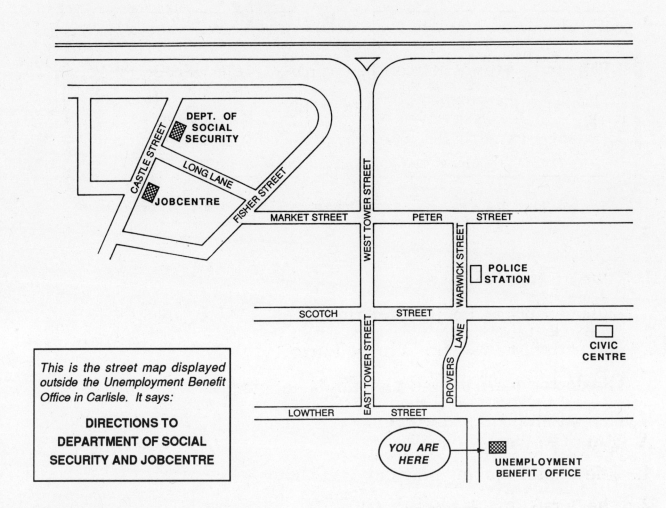

This is the street map displayed outside the Unemployment Benefit Office in Carlisle. It says:

DIRECTIONS TO DEPARTMENT OF SOCIAL SECURITY AND JOBCENTRE

Answer these questions

1. A sign on the map says YOU ARE HERE. Where is 'HERE' ?

2. In which street is the Police Station?

3. How would you direct someone from the Jobcentre to the Department of Social Security?

4. How would you direct someone from the Unemployment Benefit Office to the D.S.S.?

5. What happens at an Unemployment Benefit Office?

6. What happens at the D.S.S.?

7. What happens at the Jobcentre?

Joke

Patient	I've got this very bad pain in my right arm, doctor.
Doctor	Don't worry, it's just old age.
Patient	Well, in that case, why doesn't my left arm hurt too? I've had it just as long.

A True / False / Maybe

1. The patient has a pain in his right arm.

2. The patient has a pain in his left arm.

3. The doctor doesn't think the pain is important.

4. The patient is an old woman.

5. The doctor is a young man.

B Which word is missing?

1. I've got this very pain in my right arm.

2. Why doesn't my arm hurt too?

3. It's just old.

4. I've had it just long.

C Write these out as two words

I've

Don't

Doesn't

It's

Tablets on Prescription

> **100 CO-CODAMOL EFFERVESCENT TABLETS**
> Two to be taken four times a day
> MIX IN WATER FIRST BEFORE TAKING
> MAXIMUM 2 TABLETS PER DOSE
> MAXIMUM 8 TABLETS IN 24 HOURS

A True / False / Don't know

1. Tablets must be mixed with water.

2. Four tablets to be taken two times a day.

3. Maximum 8 tablets per dose.

4. Maximum 8 tablets in a day.

B Which word is missing?

1. Two to be four times a day.

2. Maximum tablets in 24 hours.

3. Maximum 2 per dose.

4. Mix water first before taking.

C Make these words into a sentence

day	taken	times	tablets
two	to	four	a be

Verse from a Greetings Card

Violets are red,

Roses are blue,

I'm colour blind

But I'm thinking of you!

A Which word?

1. Which words appear twice in the poem?
2. Which words contain *in* ?
3. Which word contains the word *let* ?
4. Which word is short for 'I am' ?
5. Which 2 words rhyme in the poem?

B Join the 2 halves of the words

ro	our
think	lets
vio	ses
col	ing

C Make up your own

Make up a verse of your own which begins:

Roses are red,
Violets are blue.......

Boxes in a Supermarket Warehouse

These signs all appear on cardboard storage boxes in a supermarket warehouse:

> KEEP COOL, DRY
> AND AWAY FROM
> DISINFECTANT, SOAP,
> FRUIT, CHEESE ETC.

> **IMPORTANT**
> PRODUCT MUST BE
> STORED AT -18°C / 0°F
> KEEP DEEP FROZEN

> Store below 5°C, the temperature
> in the WELL of most retail dairy cabinets

> **GLASS**
> HANDLE WITH CARE
> STORE THIS END UP
> OPEN OTHER END

A Which sign?

1. Which sign is from a box full of ice cream?
2. Which sign is from a box full of margarine tubs?
3. Which sign is from a box full of packets of tea?
4. Which sign is from a box full of wine bottles?

B Join the 2 halves of the words

fro	pen
han	tail
be	zen
pro	dle
re	duct
o	low

C Answer these questions

1. Should margarine be stored below freezing temperature?
2. Why should tea be stored away from disinfectant or soap?
3. Why should wine bottles be stored one way up but opened the other way up?
4. Where is the 'WELL' of a dairy cabinet?

Weather forecast

The Easter weekend will start off wet and cloudy. Heavy showers are expected in many areas tomorrow and on Saturday.

Sunday and Monday are expected to be drier with brighter spells, particularly in southern England and eastern Scotland.

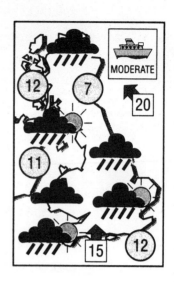

A True / False / Maybe

1. Sunday will be better than Saturday.
2. All of the UK will be wet on Saturday.
3. 'Tomorrow' in the forecast is a Friday.
4. The best weather on Monday will be in eastern Scotland.
5. There will be no weather in Wales.

B Opposites

What is the opposite of these?

wet   heavy   brighter   start   many

C Which is the odd one out?

1. tomorrow   Saturday   Sunday   Monday
2. wet   cloudy   spells   bright
3. Wales   Scotland   Northern Ireland   UK   England
4. eastern   Easter   southern   western   northern

D Make up sentences

Make up sentences which contain these pairs of words:

1. Northern Ireland   sunshine
2. Scotland   wind
3. Wales   snow
4. England   showers

Form filling

Notes:
- Please answer the questions in this booklet in ink, using CAPITAL LETTERS
- Please tick the boxes that apply

Mr ☐   Mrs ☐   Miss ☐   Ms ☐   Other ☐ → *Please specify*

Surname/Family name _____

Other names (in full) _____

Address _____

_____

_____

Postcode _____   Telephone number _____

National Insurance Number ☐ ☐ ☐ ☐ ☐

Date of birth ☐ ☐ ☐

Are you:

Single? ☐

Married? ☐

Separated? ☐

Widowed? ☐

Divorced? ☐

A   True / False / Maybe

1. You must write in capital letters

2. All the boxes should be ticked.

3. The Date of Birth should be given in words.

4. 'Surname' is the same as 'Family name'.

5. You can use a pencil to fill in the form.

6. You can use a biro to fill in the form.

7. A postcode contains both letters and numbers.

8. A National Insurance number contains both letters and numbers.

B   Fill in the form

Fill in the form for this person:

Miranda Anne Jones, 93 Bridgend Road, Birchgrove, Cardiff CF1 3ER
Tel. 0222 578427

● Which boxes would you tick for her if she had been married but was now living with another partner?

● If she was 28 last September 14th, fill in the Date of Birth box.

● What could be entered in this box?

Other ☐ → *Please specify*

Hospital sign

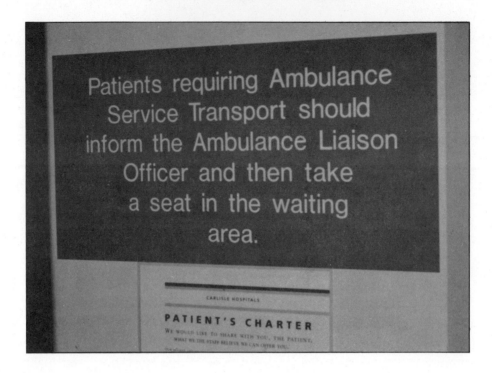

Patients requiring Ambulance Service Transport should inform the Ambulance Liaison Officer and then take a seat in the waiting area.

CARLISLE HOSPITALS

PATIENT'S CHARTER
WE WOULD LIKE TO SHARE WITH YOU, THE PATIENT, WHAT WE THE STAFF BELIEVE WE CAN OFFER YOU.

A   True / False / Maybe

1. The hospital will transport patients by ambulance.

2. The Ambulance Liaison Officer is in the waiting area.

3. The waiting area has seats.

4. The Ambulance Liaison Officer will make you wait.

5. The Ambulance Liaison Officer is a man.

6. The waiting area is full of patients.

B   How many?

1. How many words in the sign begin with a capital letter?

2. How many words in the sign begin with **t** ?

3. How many words in the sign end with **e** ?

4. How many words in the sign have **an** in them?

5. Which is the shortest word in the sign?

6. Which are the longest words in the sign?

C   Word meanings

Find a word in the sign which means the same as each of these:

tell   needing   chair

Goldfish

the scene of the crime
was a goldfish bowl
goldfish were kept
in the bowl at the time

that was the scene
and that was the crime

Alan Jackson

A Answer these questions

1. What was the crime?

2. Where did it take place?

3. Whodunnit?

4. Which lines in the poem rhyme?

B Make up your own

Make up your own version of the poem by replacing the words *goldfish* and *bowl* with other words.

Fire Extinguisher

BRITANNIA
9 litre WATER
GAS CARTRIDGE TYPE
FIRE EXTINGUISHER
TEST RATING 13A

WOOD	LIQUID	GASEOUS	ELECTRICAL
✓	✗	✗	✗

TO OPERATE

1 REMOVE
SAFETY PIN AND
UNCLIP HOSE

2 DIRECT HOSE
NOZZLE
AT BASE OF FIRE

3 SQUEEZE HANDLE
TO COMMENCE
DISCHARGE. RELEASE
TO INTERRUPT

RECHARGE AFTER COMPLETE OR PARTIAL USE
<u>WARNING</u>
**DO NOT USE ON BURNING LIQUIDS
OR LIVE ELECTRICAL EQUIPMENT**

A True / False / Maybe

1. The fire extinguisher sprays water on the fire.
2. The fire extinguisher sprays gas on the fire.
3. The fire extinguisher can be used on live electrical equipment.
4. The fire extinguisher can be used on burning plastic.
5. The fire extinguisher can be used on burning petrol.
6. The fire extinguisher can be used on burning gas.
7. The fire extinguisher won't start until the safety pin is removed.
8. The fire extinguisher jet can be stopped and started again.

B Put these instructions in the right order

Squeeze handle to commence discharge.

Recharge after use.

Unclip hose.

Direct hose nozzle at base of fire.

Release handle to interrupt discharge.

Remove safety pin.

Word puzzle

See how many words of 2 or more letters you can make from the letters in

EXTINGUISHER

Your Stars

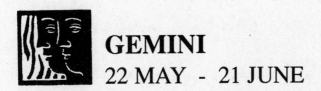

GEMINI
22 MAY - 21 JUNE

Things are looking up this week for those born under Gemini. Your social life will pick up, especially at the weekend. It's a good time for romance, too. You'll be popular with others. Money-making opportunities look good - and you can afford to take the odd risk.

A   True / False / Maybe

1. Your social life will be good at the weekend.

2. You will have a new romance.

3. Everyone born under Gemini will be popular this week.

4. You could win the Pools this week.

5. This week will be better than last.

B   Yes / No / Sometimes

1. Do you always read your 'Stars' in magazines or newspapers?

2. Do you believe everything that is said in your 'Stars'?

3. Do you think that it is all a load of rubbish?

4. Can you often think of events that agree with what is written?

5. Do you think that the people who write the 'Stars' believe in them?

C   Sort out these jumbled words from 'Your Stars'

coalis   mite   dewenek   rasts   file   yomen

D   Match the symbol with the sign

TAURUS	LIBRA	CANCER	SCORPIO	PISCES
a	b	c	d	e

Can you name the other signs of the Zodiac and give their dates?

A note on the table

Brian   4.30pm

    You Mum rang. She's had a fall and hurt her arm. I'm going to take her to hospital. Can you go and get Emma from the Sports Centre at 6 o'clock? There's some pizzas in the freezer.

        See you later — midnight?

          Kate

A   **True / False / Maybe**

1. Kate rang Brian's Mum.
2. Brian's Mum has broken her arm.
3. Emma is at the Sports Centre.
4. Brian will be home by 5.30.
5. Kate will be home at midnight.
6. The Sports Centre closes at 6 p.m.

B   **What do you think?**

1. Does Brian's Mum live on her own?
2. Is Brian's Mum elderly?
3. Do Brian and Kate live together?
4. Are Brian and Kate married?
5. What will happen if Brian is home late?
6. Is Emma Brian and Kate's daughter?
7. Does Kate usually make the tea?
8. Does Kate drive a car?
9. Are Brian and Kate both working?
10. Why does Kate say " - *midnight?*" ?

Easy chutney

MAKES 3 KILOS (6-7 LBS)

450g (1lb) stoneless dates
450g (1lb) sultanas
450g (1lb) apples
450g (1lb) onions
450g (1lb) dark brown sugar
575 ml (1 pint) vinegar
1 teaspoon salt
Ground black pepper
A dash of cayenne, allspice & ground ginger

Mince the dates, sultanas, apples and onions. Put them in a large bowl and stir in the sugar and vinegar. Add salt, pepper and spices. Leave to stand for 24 hours, giving the mixture a stir from time to time. Bottle in glass jars. This chutney is easy to make and will keep well.

from Rose Elliot's **Complete Vegetarian Cookery**

A True / False / Maybe

1. The dates have to be chopped.

2. 450g is the same as 1lb.

3. A 'dash' is more than a teaspoon.

4. The mixture needs to be stirred all the time.

5. The chutney must be cooked for 2 hours.

6. White sugar could be used for the chutney.

B What do you think?

1. How many pieces of equipment will you need for making this chutney?

2. Will the chutney be easy to make?

3. Will the chutney be cheap to make?

4. How long will it take to make the chutney?

C Opposites

All the words below appear in the recipé. Think of a word which means the opposite of each of them.

large   add   easy   dark   stoneless

Pub sign

```
The King's Arms
Relax in a real old tavern
REAL ALE
Food Served All Day
Midday - 10.00pm

❖ Morning Coffees
❖ Afternoon Teas
❖ Dish of the Day (12.00 - 3pm & 6pm - 8pm)
❖ Lunch Served 12.00 - 3pm
❖ Dinner Served 6pm - 8pm

Guest Ale of the Month
60's Music
```

A Yes / No / Don't know

1. Is food served all day?

2. Can you get food in the morning?

3. Can you get *Dish of the Day* at any time in the day?

4. Is dinner time 12 - 3 p.m.?

5. Is the King's Arms open at 10.30 a.m.?

B Answer these questions

1. What is real ale?

2. What is ale that isn't real ale?

3. The King's Arms is said to be a 'real old tavern'. How old do you think it must be to be called a 'real old tavern' - 50 years / 100 years / 200 years?

4. What is a *Guest Ale of the Month*?

5. The sign says *60's Music*. Will all the music be from the 60's?

C Complete these

Cover up all the page above this and fill in the gaps below:

1. The King's _____

2. Guest Ale of the _____

3. Dish of the _____

4. _____ served all day

5. Afternoon _____

Worming a dog

	ANIMAL	DOSE
	Puppies and small dogs 9 - 24 lbs (4 - 11 kg) e.g. Scottish terrier	5 x 1 gram sachets as a single dose or 1 x 1 gram sachet per day for 5 days
	Dogs 25 - 73 lbs (12 - 33 kg) e.g. Collie, Labrador	5 x 3 gram sachets as a single dose or 1 x 3 gram sachet per day for 5 days
	Large dogs 74 - 121 lbs (34 - 55 kg) e.g. Great Dane	8 x 3 gram sachets as a single dose or divided over 5 days

A   True / False / Maybe

1. The wormer comes in 1 gram or 3 gram sachets.
2. A sachet is a small bottle.
3. A Scottish terrier is a small dog.
4. A Collie is a large dog.
5. 24 lbs is about the same as 11 kg.
6. The wormer should be dissolved in the dog's water bowl.

B   Which is the odd one out?

1. Collie   Terrier   Puppy   Labrador
2. 24 lbs   12 kg   5 gram   5 days
3. divided   sachet   mixed   directed
4. small   single   large   great

C   Sounds

Which sound is common to all the words in each group?

1. gram   sachet   Labrador   animal
2. given   mixed   single   administration
3. administration   days   Great Dane
4. administration   divided   Labrador   directed

An inside job

A young woman went to visit a Young Offender Institution to give bible lessons. When she got back to her car she found that she had locked the keys inside it. She went back to see the Warden. He said that there were plenty of young lads inside who could get into her car. He went to ask which of the lads were in for doing cars. One of them said he was and he was taken out to the car. He picked up a brick and threw it through the windscreen!

from *The Glasgow Herald*

A   True / False / Don't know

1. The young woman gave driving lessons.
2. She had locked her bible in her car.
3. The Warden was a man.
4. All the young offenders were boys.
5. The Warden threw a brick through the windscreen.

B   Opposites

Find a word in the news item which means the opposite of each of these:

old	take	girls	opened
outside	lost	few	man

C   Sounds

1. a. How many words in the news item have a *c* sound in them (as in <u>c</u>old)?

    b. How many different ways is the *c* sound spelt?

2. *Find a word in the news item which has the same **ou** sound as each of these:*

round	tough	would	route

D   Same sound - different spelling

Think of a word which sounds the same as each of these words from the news item, but has a different spelling and meaning.

Example *(from the news item):* threw / through

to	see	there	which	for

Note from a Mail Order Company

Dear Customer,

Thank you for your order which has been sent under separate cover. The items listed below are out of stock and the refund shown is enclosed.

Code	Qty	Item	Price (inc.VAT)
H745	1	T-shirt, blue - Med.	6.99
R6381	1	Sweatshirt, red - XL	12.50
		Post & packing	-- --
		REFUND	19.49

A True / False / Maybe

1. All of the items are out of stock.
2. Red T-shirts are out of stock.
3. All red sweatshirts are out of stock.
4. The clothes are for a man.
5. Post and packing has been refunded.
6. The price included VAT.
7. The refund is in cash.

B What do you think?

1. What size was the T-shirt?
2. What size was the sweatshirt?
3. Why was there no refund of post and packing?
4. Were the clothes good value for money?
5. Is mail order a good way to buy clothes?

C Match the half sentences

The items are	your order.
The refund	been sent separately.
The order has	out of stock.
Thank you for	is enclosed.

The start of a romance

Joanne was going back to Devon because she had to. The thought of meeting Simon again had never crossed her mind!

Adam's eyes were warm with love as he kissed her goodbye through the train window.

"Have a good journey, darling," he said.

They had driven to the station in silence. They both had things that they wanted to say but they didn't say them. Silences, she thought, are often worse than arguments. At least you know where you are with an argument.......

based on a story from a women's magazine

A   Yes / No / Perhaps

1. Is Adam going on the train with Joanne?
2. Is Joanne in love with Adam?
3. Is Simon an old friend of Joanne's?
4. Are Adam and Joanne married?
5. Have Adam and Joanne had a lot of arguments?

B   Tell someone else or write the answers

1. What does Joanne look like?
2. What does Adam look like?
3. What does Simon look like?
4. What do you think will happen in the story?
5. Will the story have a happy ending?

C   Word meanings

1. *Find words in the story which mean the opposite of each of these:*

   cold   bad   hate   hello   better

2. *All of the words below appear in the story. Think of a word which means the same as each of them.*

   argument   silence   darling   journey   wanted

Deter mice and rats

To help rid yourself of rats or mice, just plug in the Rodent Repeller. The economical small twin-speaker unit makes a continuous sweep of 130 decibel sound waves. These  cannot be heard by humans but can help send most pests packing, without harm! One unit should protect an unobstructed indoor area of around 3,500 square feet. Complete with mains transformer. Won't affect pets except small rodents.

Rodent Repeller   *£19.99 (including post & packing)*

A   Answer these questions

1. Does the Repeller kill mice and rats?
2. Will the Repeller be noisy?
3. Will the Repeller affect cats or dogs?
4. Will the Repeller affect a pet hamster?
5. Will 1 Repeller keep a whole house free of mice?
6. Do you think there are any moving parts in it?
7. Does the Repeller work off a battery or the mains?
8. Do you think it is good value at £19.99?
9. Do you think it will work?
10. Do they say that it gets rid of all mice and rats?

B   What is wrong?

Spot the error in each of these sentences.

1. The Repeller will help rid you of rats and mince.
2. The unit makes a sweep of 130 decidel sound waves.
3. The sound waves send most pets packing.
4. One unit should protest an area of around 3,500 square feet.
5. Complete with mans transformer.
6. Won't affect pests except small rodents.
7. Deter rice and mats.

Advert for Pop Group Tour

BLAGGERS I★T★A

THE UNITED COLOURS OF FRUSTRATION TOUR

WITH BLADE & FUN-DA-MENTAL

MAY	2ND	BRISTOL, FLEECE & FIRKIN
	6TH	BIRMINGHAM, EDWARDS No.8
	8TH	LONDON, KENNINGTON PARK 'JOBS NOT RACISM' FESTIVAL
	9TH	CARDIFF, UNIVERSITY
	14TH	LEEDS, UNIVERSITY
	15TH	GLASGOW, CATHOUSE
	20TH	OXFORD, VENUE
	21ST	WINDSOR, OLD TROUT
	22ND	HARLOW, SQUARE
	27TH	LONDON, U.L.U.
	28TH	SALISBURY, ARTS CENTRE
	29TH	BRIGHTON, MADEIRA HOTEL

BLAGGERS I.T.A. ALSO APPEARING AT:

MAY	1ST	LONDON, THE DOME, TUFNELL PARK
	13TH	LEICESTER, PRINCESS CHARLOTTE
	16TH	DERBY, WHEREHOUSE

OUT JUNE 1ST
THE DEBUT PARLOPHONE SINGLE 'STRESSS'
7" WHITE VINYL, 12', CD & TAPE.

BLAGGERS ITA / ANTI-FASCIST ACTION
BM BOX 1734, LONDON WC1N 3XX

from New Musical Express

A Which is the odd one out?

1. OXFORD   LEEDS   GLASGOW   WINDSOR

2. 14TH   20TH   21ST   28TH

3. BRISTOL   DERBY   BRIGHTON   BIRMINGHAM

4. FLEECE & FIRKIN   MADEIRA HOTEL   UNIVERSITY   OLD TROUT

B Capital letters

Write these in your own handwriting, only using capital letters where they are needed:

MAY   ARTS CENTRE   ALSO   SALISBURY   OLD TROUT

APPEARING   CARDIFF   OUT   BLAGGERS I.T.A.

C Which place?

Say which place on the tour would be nearest to each of the places below.

1. Newcastle-upon-Tyne
2. Shrewsbury
3. Portsmouth
4. Ipswich
5. Exeter
6. Stockport

Finding a playgroup

If you are looking for a playgroup, nursery or infant school:

O Go to see the playgroup or school. See a few if you have a choice. Talk to the people in charge, look at what's going on, ask questions.

O Trust your feelings. If you like the feel of a place, and the children seem happy and busy, that's a good sign.

O Talk to other parents whose children are at the group or school. Your health visitor may also be able to tell you about it.

O Talk about ways of getting your child to settle in at first.

based on part of Health Education booklet **Birth to Five**

A Agree / Disagree / Not sure / Other

1. Playgroups are good for children.

2. Playgroups are good for mothers.

3. The people in charge always know what's best.

4. The happiest playgroups are the most untidy.

5. A playgroup is the same as a nursery.

B Find the right word

Without looking at the top of the page, choose the right word from the box to fill each of the gaps in the sentences below.

| like | have | see | good |
| talk | look | hear | looking |

1. If you are _____ for a playgroup or infant school, go to _____ the group or school.

2. See a few if you _____ a choice.

3. _____ at what's going on.

4. If you _____ the feel of a place, that's a _____ sign.

5. _____ to other parents at the group or school.

Yellow Pages

*These are some of the firms listed under **Drain & pipe cleaning** in the Cumbria and North Lancashire **Yellow Pages**:*

1A DYNO-SERVICES

DYNO·SERVICES R

THE UK'S NO 1 DRAIN CLEANER
FAST 24HR LOCAL SERVICE
Carlisle 591888 / Barrow-in-F 821753
Lancaster 848999
Workington 871811
H.O.143 Maple Rd,Surbiton,Surrey

1 A Metro-Rod, The Old Rectory	Kirklinton	75065
Andidrain, 71 Hurley Rd,Little Corby	Carlisle	39037
Angus R.F, 28 Etterby Lea Crescent	Carlisle	42974
Drainaway, 1 Rennie Court,Haverbreaks	Lancaster	844877
Dyno-Rod plc—		
577-587 Harehills Lane,Leeds	Carlisle	591888
	Barrow-in-F	821753
	Kendal	733711
	Workington	871811
Astra Business Centre,180 Longridge Rd, Preston	Lancaster	848999
Mike's Drain Cleaning,		
78 Newlands Gardens	Workington	67208

MIKES DRAINS

LOW COST
Domestic & Industrial Drain Cleaning
FREE 30 MIN CCTV SURVEY
IF JETTED
FREE 24 HR. CALL OUT
78 Newlands Gardens, Workington
(0900) 67208

APOLLO DRAINS
WINDERMERE
05394 32044

DRAIN JETTING, CCTV SURVEYS

SEPTIC TANK INSTALLATIONS,
GUTTERS & DOWN PIPES GENERAL
PLUMBING REPAIRS

OLD WESLEYAN CHAPEL,
RYDAL ROAD,
AMBLESIDE

BURST PIPES

DRAIN-SCAN

- DOMESTIC DRAIN CLEARANCE
- REMOTE COLOUR CCTV SURVEYS
- ELECTRONIC DRAIN LOCATION
- 24 HOUR SERVICE

(0524) 859515

NEWFIELD HOUSE, MIDDLETON ROAD, HEYSHAM

A   Which firms are listed for:

1. Lancaster?
2. Carlisle?
3. Workington?
4. Ambleside?

B   Answer these questions

1. Is *1A Dyno-Services* the same as **1A Metro-Rod**?
2. Is *1A Dyno-Services* the same as **Dyno-Rod plc**?
3. What does 'H.O.' stand for in the *1A Dyno-Services* advertisement?
4. What is the dialling code for Heysham in Lancashire?
5. How many of the firms look as if they could be 'one-man' businesses?
6. How many times does the word **drain** appear in the above item?

Hospital appointment

OUT-PATIENT APPOINTMENT

An appointment has been made for you to be seen by:-

    MR. D. FOOT   or colleague

on:- THURSDAY THE 1ST OF APRIL

at:- 9.50 A.M.

When you arrive you should first report to the reception desk. Please bring any appointment cards you may have. If ambulance transport has been arranged for you please try to be ready from 8.30 am. for morning appointments and 12.30 pm. for afternoon appointments regardless of appointment time.

If it is impossible for you to attend it is important that you notify us as soon as possible so that another patient may have the opportunity to be seen. We will do our best to offer you a more convenient appointment.

On your first visit please bring a note of any tablets/medicine you may be taking.

NEW PATIENT

A True / False / Maybe

1. The appointment is for the out-patient department.

2. You will be seen by Mr. B. Foot.

3. You do not need an appointment card.

4. The ambulance will arrive at 8.30 p.m.

5. You can change your appointment.

6. You should bring any tablets you are taking.

B Word meanings

All the words below appear in the letter. Think of a word which means the same as each of them.

    arranged   notify   attend   opportunity   offer

C An out-patient's word puzzle

While you wait for your appointment, see how many words of 2 or more letters you can make from the letters in each of these words:

INFIRMARY   **APPOINTMENT**   **TABLETS**

Catherine Cookson

Catherine Cookson is known and loved by a large public through her vibrant and earthy novels set in and around the North-East of England, past and present. In **Our Kate** we see how it is that she knows her background and characters so well.

The 'Our Kate' of the title is not Catherine Cookson but her mother, around whom the autobiography revolves. **Our Kate** is a true story about living with hardship and poverty, seen through the eyes of the sensitive child and woman who won through to become Catherine Cookson, the warm and human writer we know today.

based on the cover blurb for **Our Kate** *by Catherine Cookson*

A   True / False / Maybe

1. The book is Catherine Cookson's life story.
2. 'Our Kate' is Catherine Cookson.
3. The author was born in North-East England.
4. Catherine Cookson writes novels.
5. Catherine Cookson was a sensitive child.
6. An autobiography is a true story.
7. 'Vibrant' means 'cruel'.

B   Answer these questions

1. What are novels?
2. What is the difference between an autobiography and a biography?
3. Where can you find the 'blurb' in a book? What is it?
4. What is fiction? Give the titles of 3 fiction books.
5. What is non fiction? Give the titles of 3 non fiction books.

C   Finish the pairs

Examples (from the passage):   past and present;   in and around

night and _____   now and _____

hot and _____   cut and _____

free and _____   high and _____

by and _____   give and _____

time and _____   here and _____

Housing Benefit form

DO YOU LIVE IN:	✓		✓		✓		✓
Room(s) in part of a house		Flat over a shop		Bungalow		{ Detached	
Flat in part of a house		Maisonette		House		{ Semi-detached	
Flat in a block of flats		Hostel		A caravan or mobile home		{ Terraced	

Please complete in all circumstances	Bedrooms	Bedsitter	Kitchen	Bathroom	Living/ Dining	Other rooms
The number of rooms in the house						
The number of rooms for your use						
The number of rooms shared with people not in your household						
How many floors are there in the whole house?		Which floor(s) do you live on?				
Is your room at the	Front		Middle		Rear	of the Property
Is any part of your property used for business purposes?	YES		NO			

PROOF: I WILL NEED TO SEE PROOF OF THE AMOUNT YOU PAY. PLEASE SEND ME YOUR TENANCY AGREEMENT AND RENT BOOK, RECEIPTS, OR A LETTER FROM YOUR LANDLORD/LADY OR AGENT.

A True / False / Maybe

1. A bedsitter is 'a room in part of a house'.

2. A bungalow is not a house.

3. A flat is different from a maisonette.

4. A bungalow can be semi-detached.

5. 3 or more houses joined together is a terrace.

B Fill in the form

Fill in the form for yourself

or

Fill in the form for a person who lives in a bedsitter at the back of the middle floor of a 3-storey house. Decide for yourself any other details that are asked for.

C Words from words

Make as many words as you can with 2 or more letters in them using the letters in

MAISONETTE

The Card for Life

If you carry a donor card it means that you want some parts of your body to be used as transplants after your death to help others live. Six parts of the body can be used - kidneys, heart, lungs, liver, cornea and pancreas. After death, a machine keeps the blood circulating until the organs are removed. This stops them decaying. The body is not disfigured and a normal funeral can take place. You should always make sure that everyone in your family knows that you carry a card.

from a Department of Health leaflet

A Which is which?

Match the parts of the body with the diagrams:

| kidneys | heart | lungs | cornea | liver | pancreas |

a   b   c   d   e   f

B Yes / No / Maybe

1. Everyone should carry a donor card.
2. The eye can be used as a transplant.
3. The organs are removed before death.
4. A normal funeral can take place.
5. All your friends should know about your donor card.

C Put these jumbled sentences in the right order

1. around heart The blood body the pumps.
2. others card a donor helps live to Carrying.
3. the parts of Six be body can used.
4. After a place funeral take death can normal.
5. two There kidneys in body and lungs the two are.

D Word beginnings (Prefixes)

Make a list of words which have the same beginning (prefix) as these:

1. **trans**plants
2. **circ**ulating
3. **dis**figured
4. **de**caying

Local News item

Handbag snatch foiled

A brave woman clung on to her handbag and forced her attacker to flee when she was stopped on the Norcot Road, Reading, on Monday.

The 39-year-old was passing the dental surgery just before 6 pm when the teenager struck, running up to her and trying to snatch the bag from her shoulder.

She refused to let go and the would-be robber fled on foot towards the Dee Road estate.

Police are appealing for information regarding a youth aged about 17, who was wearing a black sweatshirt and red baseball cap.

*from the **Reading Chronicle***

A True / False / Maybe

1. The woman had been to the dentist.
2. The attacker was 39 years old.
3. The attack happened on Monday afternoon.
4. The teenager wore a red baseball cap.
5. The teenager was from the Dee Road estate.
6. The teenager was a male.

B Choose the right word

1. Her attacker was forced to _____ . (*flea* / *flee* / *flew*)
2. She refused _____ let go. (*two* / *too* / *to*)
3. He tried to snatch the bag _____ her shoulder. (*from* / *form* / *for*)
4. He was _____ a black sweatshirt. (*warning* / *wearing* / *worrying*)
5. The _____ - be robber fled on foot. (*wood* / *could* / *would*)

C Finish these sentences in your own words

1. The woman was.....
2. The attack happened.....
3. The teenager should.....
4. The police will.....
5. Newspapers always.....

Wall Tile Spacers

To space tiles evenly

1.
Snap off individual spacers.

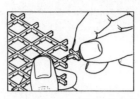

2.
Fix first tile squarely in position and place a spacer at each corner. (Individual legs of spacers can be broken off to give T or L shapes for edges and corners.)

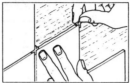

3.
Fix next tile alongside, and place spacers at corners.

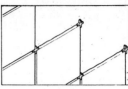

4.
Continue until all tiles have been fixed.
Leave at least 24 hours for adhesive to set and then grout tile joints, leaving spacers in position.

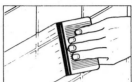

A Put these instructions in the right order

Place a spacer at each corner.

Grout tile joints after at least 24 hours.

Fix next tile alongside.

Place a spacer at each corner.

Fix first tile squarely in position.

Snap off individual spacers.

Continue until all tiles have been fixed.

B Answer these questions

1. Where would you use an L shape wall tile spacer?

2. Will the spacers help to give a smooth, flat wall surface?

3. Will the spacers show after the wall is finished?

4. Will you need 4 spacers for every tile on the wall?

5. Do you think it is easy to tile a wall?

C Find another word

*In the following instructions, replace the word in **bold** print with another one which means much the same.*

1. Fix **next** tile alongside.

2. Individual **legs** of spacers can be broken off.

3. Leave at least 24 hours for adhesive to **set**.

4. **Snap** off the individual spacers.

5. Fix first tile squarely in **position**.

*Brown and Brown / **Reading Worksheets***

Hollywood Bowl

FABULOUS FUN FOR ALL THE FAMILY

HOORAY FOR HOLLYWOOD
A real fun packed family experience, 24 lanes with the very latest computer assisted scoring, that's entertainment 90's style. It's fun ... it's entertaining ... it's ten pin bowling - Hollywood Bowl Style.

HOLLYWOOD DINER
For the hungry bowlers, check out our easy diner. A mouth watering menu that'll give you high energy for more of that Hollywood Bowling.

CUE 147
Take a break from Hollywood Bowling at Cue 147. Nine full size snooker tables for pot shots and professionals alike. It's easy on the pocket!

CANDY STRIKE
Pick & Mix sweets plus a range of pro equipment for bowlers of all ages.

BOWL BUDDIES
A sure way to score for children and beginners. Two inflatable tubes fill the gutters and keep the ball on course for the pins. A sure winner!

DI MAGGIO'S BAR
Say cheers in the atmosphere of Di Maggio's Bar. The perfect venue for a pre-bowl drink or to relax with friends after your game.

GIANT'S DEN PLAY AREA
Super safety zone for the under 5's who find that their bowling Mums and Dads get on top of their feet.

A Numbers

Make a list of all the numbers *(words and figures)* in the advertisement for Hollywood Bowl.

B Answer these questions

1. Where can you get something to eat?

2. Is there an automatic scoring system for the bowls?

3. Can you take young children along with you?

4. What help is there for beginner bowlers?

5. How many pins are there to aim at?

6. Why is the snooker section called *Cue 147* ?

C Headings

Look at the 7 headings in capital letters.

1. Which American words are used in the headings?

2. What English word could be used for each American word?

Scrabble inventor dies

The man who invented *Scrabble*, the world's most popular spelling game, died in April 1993 in New York at the age of 93. Alfred Butts invented *Scrabble* in 1931 but it was over 20 years before it really caught on. The owner of a New York department store got hooked on the game in 1952 and within a year it had become a national craze.

Alfred Butts was not very good at *Scrabble* himself because he was a poor speller! He worked out the values of the letter tiles by counting the number of times each letter appeared on the front page of the *New York Times*. He made up sets of the game in his garage and sold them to local people. At first, the game was called *Criss-Cross*, then *Lexico* and it only became *Scrabble* in 1948. He made very little money out of his invention but he was quite well off, having spent his life as an architect.

A   True / False / Maybe

1. The inventor of *Scrabble* was called Alfred Butts.

2. Alfred Butts was born in 1900.

3. The game was invented in 1913.

4. Alfred Butts was a poor speller.

5. The game was first called *Lexico*.

6. *Scrabble* is the world's best-selling game.

B   How many endings?

How many endings can you add to these words?

1. invent

2. spell

3. call

4. depart

C   Longest word

What is the longest word you can make from these sets of letters?

1. S F M I E H L

2. R L E L E S P

3. S B U E E C A

4. R P U L A P O

Unemployment Benefit Declaration

Declaration

I understand that if I knowingly give information that is incorrect or incomplete, action may be taken against me.

I claim Unemployment Benefit and declare that:

- the answers to the questions in parts 1, 2 and 3 are true and complete and that I will tell the Employment Service of any changes;

- I have read and understood the booklet UB40/UBL18 'Information for Clients';

- I am unemployed, available for, able to work, and intend to actively seek employment; and

- on each day from and including the date shown on page 1, I have been unemployed, available for, able and willing to do and actively seeking work, but have been unable to get any.

*Please do **not** sign this until you are asked to do so at your interview*	
Signed	**Date**

Please tick this box if someone else filled in this form for you. ☐

Declaration from Benefit Claim Form ES461

A True / False / Maybe

1. There are 3 parts to the form.

2. The Declaration is a legal statement.

3. You have to read the booklet before you can sign the form.

4. You must be out of work to get Unemployment Benefit.

5. You must look for work to get Unemployment Benefit.

6. If you give the wrong information, you could be taken to Court.

7. You should sign the form before you go to the interview.

8. You can get someone else to sign the form.

B Choose the right beginning

*Each of the words below begins either with **un** or with **in**. Choose the right beginning for each word.*

___ able   ___ formation   ___ tend   ___ derstand

___ cluding   ___ correct   ___ employment   ___ derstood

___ complete   ___terview

Video cover

RICHARD ATTENBOROUGH'S FILM

CHAPLIN

The cast of the film **Chaplin** reads like a *Who's Who* of screen talent. Richard Attenborough's much-praised film tells the story of the life and times of one of the cinema's most famous names - Charlie Chaplin.

It's a journey through the thrills and spills, the laughter and the sorrow that made up Chaplin's life behind and in front of the camera. The film follows his life through his early days of poverty in London; his first steps towards success in the music-hall; his beginnings as a film actor and then his days as director and star of some of the greatest films in the history of the cinema.

With Robert Downey Jr's dazzling performance as Chaplin, this is one film you don't want to miss.

based on the cover blurb of a Guild Home Video

A Yes / No / Don't know

1. Is the film called *Charlie Chaplin*?
2. Is Richard Attenborough the director of the film?
3. Was Charlie Chaplin born in London?
4. Did Chaplin direct films as well as act in them?
5. Was Chaplin a failure as a music-hall artist?
6. Was Chaplin a comedy actor?

B Opposites

Give a word which means the opposite of each of these:

famous   poverty   success   beginnings   sorrow   miss

C Finish these sentences

1. Richard Attenborough's film.....
2. Charlie Chaplin was.....
3. Chaplin's films are.....
4. Certificate 15 for a film means.....
5. Films on video are.....

Reducing the risk of cot death

Cot Death is more common in babies who go to sleep on their tummies. Babies should be laid down to sleep:

A) on their backs **or** **B)** on their sides, with the lower arm forward to stop rolling over.

Don't be worried that babies might be sick or choke if laid on their backs. This does not seem to happen. For babies who have been used to sleeping on their tummies, try them on their back or side, but do not force them if they do not like the change. Make sure that your family, baby-sitters or childminders all know about this advice.

from Department of Health Leaflet BTS 1/E

A True / False / Maybe

1. The box on the right says 'ACK TO SLEEP'.

2. Babies should be laid on their backs.

3. Babies should never be laid on their tummies.

4. Babies will not be sick if laid on their backs.

5. Babies can be laid on their sides.

6. Cot deaths never happen when babies are laid on their backs.

B Choose the spelling

Choose one of the spellings in the box to complete the words below. All the words must be found in the item about cot deaths above.

ch	sl	sh	th

_ _ em   _ _ eir   _ _ eeping   _ _ at

_ _ oke   _ _ ildminders   _ _ is   _ _ ould

C Finish these sentences in your own words

1. If babies are laid on their sides, you should........

2. Make sure that your family and baby-sitters........

3. Cot Deaths happen more often when........

4. The best way for babies to sleep is........

Letter from Bank Manager

Dear Mr. & Mrs. MacDonald,

At the close of business on January 14th your current account was £135 overdrawn.

If you consider that an overdraft facility would be of assistance, I should be pleased to discuss this with you. Alternatively we shall assume, if we do not hear from you within the next 10 days, that you will be paying in sufficient money to clear your overdraft.

As a result of the additional work involved we shall be making a charge of £18. This will be debited to your account at the time of the next quarterly charges.

I look forward to hearing from you.

Yours sincerely,

Mrs. M.K. O'Leary
Manager

A True / False / Maybe

1. The MacDonalds' account is overdrawn.
2. The MacDonalds do not have an overdraft facility.
3. The bank wants to give them an overdraft facility.
4. If they pay £150 into their account at once, there will be no charges.
5. They get quarterly charges on their account.

B Word meanings

Find a word in the letter which means much the same as each of these words:

think   help   or   enough   extra

C Join up these half sentences

We shall be making	to hearing from you.
I should be pleased	was £135 overdrawn.
I look forward	a charge of £18.
Your current account	to discuss this with you.

Hotel advertisement

The Tudor Rose Hotel, St. Nicholas Street, off Tuesday Market Place, King's Lynn, Norfolk PE30 1LR

from English Tourist Board booklet Let's Go!

Owner-run, timbered, town-centre hotel. 15th C beamed restaurant and real ale bars. Vegetarian, local fish, seafood, steaks and game. Restaurant, bars. Dogs by arrangement.
£69.00 for midweek breaks
1 September 1992 - 31 March 1993 and
1 April 1993 - 30 September 1993
Price not applicable: Christmas and New Year.
Price includes: accommodation for any two nights, breakfast, dinner and VAT per person sharing a double room.
Tel. (0553) 762824 Fax: (0553) 764894

True / False / Maybe

1. The Tudor Rose Hotel is in Tuesday Market Place.
2. The Hotel is run by the owner.
3. The bars all have 15th Century beams.
4. Dogs can be accommodated in the Hotel.
5. The food is all vegetarian.

What's in the price?

1. Does the price include breakfast?
2. Does the price include lunch?
3. Does the price include dinner?
4. Does the price pay for 2 nights at a weekend?
5. Does the price increase after March 31st?
6. How much would it cost for 2 people for 2 nights?

Join up these half words

rest	mas
arrange	ation
in	arian
Christ	aurant
sea	cludes
veget	food
accommod	ment

Recipé from a Pasta packet

PASTA AND BACON CASSEROLE
SERVES 4

225g (8 oz) Pasta Twists
600ml (1 pint) fresh tomato juice
made from 900g (2 lbs) ripe tomatoes
- see method for details
1 large onion, finely grated
salt and pepper
1/4 x 5 ml tsp. caraway seeds
4-6 bacon rashers, diced
100g (4 oz) grated Cheddar cheese

1. Cook the pasta twists in boiling water for 10-12 minutes until 'al dente'. Drain well and toss in a knob of butter or a little olive oil.

2. Blanch tomatoes in boiling water and remove skins. Place tomatoes in a liquidiser or blender and blend to a fine pulp.

3. Combine tomato juice, onion, salt and pepper and caraway seeds in a flameproof casserole dish and bring slowly to the simmer.

4. In another pan, fry the bacon in its own fat.

5. Preheat oven to 200°C, 400°F, Gas Mark 6.

6. Add pasta to sauce.

7. Add half of the grated cheese and the bacon. Stir well.

8. Sprinkle remaining cheese on top.

9. Cook in the oven for 25 minutes and serve at once.

Answer these questions

1. Pasta comes from: Spain / Italy / France / Germany?

2. What items of equipment will be needed for cooking and serving this recipé?

3. What is the 'method'?

4. What time of year would be best for making this dish?

5. What is the difference between a liquidiser and a blender?

6. What is a flameproof casserole dish?

7. How long do you think it would take to make this recipé?

8. Could a vegetarian use this recipé?

9. Do you think this is an easy recipé?

AIDS / HIV

AIDS is caused by a virus called HIV. HIV damages the body's defence system so that it cannot fight other infections. Sometimes people live for many years with HIV but others may get a fatal disease quite quickly. HIV is not passed on through everyday social contact. It is passed on in 3 main ways:

- ❑ through unprotected sexual intercourse
- ❑ by drug users sharing needles
- ❑ by a mother with HIV infecting her unborn baby

It is possible for HIV to be passed on by contact with another person's blood. However, in this country (and most others) all blood products are tested and you cannot get HIV from blood or blood products in hospital. You should avoid sharing toothbrushes or razors.

You cannot get HIV by shaking hands or hugging a person with HIV. You cannot get HIV by sharing objects like cups, cutlery, glasses, food, clothes, toilet seats or door knobs. HIV has been found in saliva but it is thought unlikely that the virus could be passed on by kissing or through tears or sweat.

A   True / False / Maybe

1. You can get HIV from sharing drug needles.
2. You can get HIV from sharing someone else's glass.
3. You cannot get HIV from another person's blood.
4. You can get HIV from kissing.
5. You can get HIV from protected sexual intercourse.
6. HIV is a fatal disease.
7. People with HIV always die very quickly.
8. You can get HIV from sharing someone's toothbrush.
9. HIV is a virus.
10. A mother with AIDS always passes it on to her baby.

B   Syllables

How many syllables are there in these words? The first three are done for you.

prod + ucts *(2)*	the *(1)*	sal + i + va *(3)*
that	hospital	contact
others	damages	toothbrushes
caused	razors	fight
unprotected	infections	everyday

100 years of films

Films have now been around for about 100 years. The first films were shown in the 1890s. It is thought that the first time that the public paid to see a film was in 1895 in the Grand Café in Paris. In the next year, 1896, the first film was shown in Britain at the Regent Street Polytechnic in London. The first Hollywood film was made in 1910, but all films were silent until 1927. Until that date, cinemas had a piano player who would play whilst keeping up with the action on the screen.

The first talking film was *The Jazz Singer* in which Al Jolson said the words "You ain't heard nothing yet!". Walt Disney first used stereo sound in 1940, but high quality sound for films did not come in until *Star Wars* in 1977. Nowadays, films are made for TV and video as well as for the cinema.

You must remember this...
Bergman and Bogart in
which film?

A   True / False / Maybe

1. The first film was made in 1890.
2. The Grand Café is in London.
3. Al Jolson was a singer.
4. All films were silent until 1927.
5. Walt Disney was the first person to use stereo sound.
6. *Star Wars* was made for TV.

B   Which is the odd word out?

1. keeping   talking   shown   nothing
2. player   actor   singer   writer
3. cinema   café   street   Polytechnic
4. London   Paris   Britain   Hollywood
5. screen   silent   video   stereo

C   Look through quickly

Answer these questions by looking quickly through the passage:

1. How many place names are there?
2. How many dates are there?
3. How many words begin with capital letters?
4. How many times do the words *film* or *films* appear?
5. How many sentences are there?
6. Which sentences do **not** contain the word *first* ?

Restart interview letter

Dear Mrs. Ling,

CLAIMANT ADVISER SERVICE - HELPING YOU INTO EMPLOYMENT

An appointment has been made for you to attend an interview with a Claimant Adviser.

The appointment has been made for

Wednesday 5th November at 12.15 pm

at the office named at the top of this letter.

Please bring with you your signing booklet (UB40/UBL18) and any evidence of your efforts to find work.

People who do not attend employment interviews without giving a good reason could lose their entitlement to benefit and/or National Insurance credits.

If you cannot attend the interview please let us know either by telephoning the number at the top of this letter, or notifying us in writing before the appointment date.

At the interview we will refund your travel costs if this appointment does not coincide with your normal signing place and you travel by the cheapest available means.

We look forward to seeing you.

for MANAGER

A   True / False / Maybe

1.   The interview is on the first Wednesday in November.

2.   The interview is in the morning.

3.   Mrs. Ling has to see the Claimant Adviser.

4.   She has to take her UB40 card with her.

5.   If she doesn't go they will stop her benefits.

6.   They will refund her travel costs.

7.   She can choose the way she travels to the interview.

8.   She can cancel the interview at any time.

9.   They look forward to seeing her.

10.   She looks forward to seeing them.

Instructions for a Microwave

1. Push the **PUSH TO OPEN** button.	
2. Place the food, or food in its container, on the Turntable Tray.	
3. Close the door. The latch will snap shut, automatically locking the door. If the door is not closed properly, the oven will not start.	
4. Set the Oven Control, as instructed on the next pages, "HOW TO SET THE OVEN CONTROL".	
5. Touch the **START** button.	The Oven will start cooking, and the Fan, Turntable, Oven Light, and Cook Indicator display will come on.
6. End of Cooking Cycle: 1) The Timer switches off.	The beeper will sound three times. The oven will automatically shut off, and the Fan, Turntable, Oven Light, the Cook Indicator Display will turn off, and the Clock will reappear on the display.
2) Open the door during cooking.	The oven will automatically shut off. The Fan, Turntable and Oven Light will turn off and the Cook Indicator Display will stop at the cooking time remaining. The oven will not restart until the door is closed and the **START** button is pushed again.
3) Touch **CLEAR** button during cooking.	The oven will automatically turn off; the Fan, Turntable, Oven Light and the Cook Indicator Display will turn off. To resume cooking the Oven must be reset.

A Yes / No / Don't know

1. Will the beeper sound 3 times when you open the door?

2. Should you place food without a container on the turntable?

3. Does the oven start automatically when you close the door?

4. If you open the door during cooking, do you have to press the **START** button again to restart the oven?

5. If you touch the **CLEAR** button during cooking, do you have to reset the Oven Control?

B What do you think?

1. If you could only have one type of oven, which would you choose?

   a) a microwave oven   **b)** a gas oven   **c)** an electric oven

2. What advantages, if any, are there in using a microwave oven?

3. Does food cooked in a microwave taste different from food cooked in a normal oven or pan?

4. Are there any dangers in using a microwave oven?

Dying to dye?

With little more than a packet of Dylon dye, you can transform anything from a shirt to a whole wardrobe into a completely new look.

The amount of dye required depends on the <u>DRY</u> weight of the item you wish to dye. The weight guide on the left indicates how much each pack will dye to achieve the strongest shade and gives examples of the more commonly dyed items.

By Hand
For up to 250g/8ozs - 1 pack x Dylon Hand

By Machine
For up to 500g/1lb - 1 pack x Dylon Machine

When using Dylon Machine the weight of the fabric to be dyed should not exceed half the machine's maximum load.

Weight Guide

T-shirt	150g/ 5oz		Double sheet (poly/cotton)	800g/29oz
Shirt	250g/ 8oz		Single sheet (poly/cotton)	600g/21oz
Jeans	700g/25oz		Bath Towel	550g/20oz
Blouse	150g/ 5oz		Hand Towel	300g/11oz
Cotton Jumper	500g/ 1lb		Duvet Cover (double)	1000g/36oz
Sweatshirt	300g/11oz		Bedspread (double)	1750g/62oz
Trousers (lightweight cotton)	250g/ 9oz		Large Tablecloth	700g/25oz
Bra	75g/ 3oz			
Briefs	50g/ 2oz			
Petticoat	100g/ 4oz			

All weights shown are approximate.

A How many and how much?

1. *Using **Dylon Hand**:*

   a. How many T shirts can you dye with one pack?

   b. How many pairs of briefs can you dye with one pack?

   c. How many packs would you need to dye a pair of jeans?

   d. How many packs would you need to dye a shirt and trousers the same colour?

2. *Using **Dylon Machine**:*

   a. What is the largest single item you could dye with one pack?

   b. How many of the smallest item could you dye with one pack?

   c. How much dye is needed to dye a duvet cover and a double sheet the same colour?

   d. How much dye is needed to dye a bath towel and a hand towel the same colour?

   e. If your washing machine's maximum load is 9 lbs, could you dye a double bedspread?

B Word meanings

Find a word in the instructions above which means much the same as each of these:

needed   change   cloth   shows   largest   deepest

Index